DARK
ENTRIES

WRITER
IAN RANKIN

ART
WERTHER DELL'EDERA

LETTERS
CLEM ROBINS

DARK
ENTRIES

DARK ENTRIES
VERTIGO CRIME

DARK ENTRIES Published by DC Comics, 1700 Broadway, New York, NY 10019. Copyright

© 2009 by DC Comics. All rights reserved. VERTIGO, VERTIGO CRIME and all characters,

the distinctive likenesses thereof and all related elements are trademarks of DC Comics.

The stories, characters and incidents mentioned in this book are entirely fictional.

DC Comics does not read or accept unsolicited submissions of ideas, stories or artwork.

Printed in the U.S.A. First Printing. DC Comics, a Warner Bros. Entertainment Company.

ISBN: 978-1-4012-2429-5

Certified Chain of Custody
60% Certified Fiber Sourcing and
40% Post-Consumer Recycled
www.sfiprogram.org

NSF-SFICOC-C0001801

This label applies to the text stock

ANYTOWN, ENGLAND.

TV CHEF'S PORN SHAME

I BUY A PAPER ON REFLEX.

NO NEWS INSIDE, JUST SYNAPSE-NUMBING JUNK.

SAME GOES FOR THE WHISKEY: REFLEX, THAT'S ALL.

THE TOP MODEL FELL FOR HIS ROCK STAR LOOKS...

NOT TO MENTION HIS MILLIONS.

SYNAPSE-NUMBING, TOO.

HIGLAND PARK ESTᴰ 1978
SINGLE MALT SCOTCH WHISKY
AGED 18 YEARS

"HIS HEAVY DRUG USE WAS NO BARRIER TO THEIR FIRST NIGHT OF PASSION."

IN A FIVE-STAR HOTEL SUITE.

YOU *WOULD* THOUGH, WOULDN'T YOU? IF HE ASKED?

BLOODY BUS. I'M GOING TO MISS "WORST CELEBRITY DRIVERS."

IT'S REPEATED LATER. EVERYTHING'S REPEATS THESE DAYS.

ANYTHING TO ERASE THE JABBER.

7

AN ENGLISHMAN'S HOME IS HIS CASTLE.

EVEN WHEN IT'S *NOT*.

DRAWBRIDGE DOWN, PORTCULLIS BREACHED.

9

11

DON'T MIND IF I SMOKE, DO YOU?

I STOPPED A FEW YEARS BACK, BUT LIKE WATCHING OTHERS DO IT. PUFF AWAY.

THANKS. BY THE WAY, DO YOU KNOW FRANCIS BACON?

HE WAS AN ARTIST. GUY BROKE INTO HIS STUDIO ONE NIGHT AND THE TWO ENDED UP BEST MATES. MIGHT *NOT* HAPPEN TO US.

I'M IN TELEVISION, MR. CONSTANTINE. THE COMPANY I WORK FOR PRODUCES SOME OF BRITAIN'S MOST WATCHED PROGRAMS.

12

OUR FIRST SUCCESS WAS WITH A *CHEF*, SADLY NOW OF SOME NOTORIETY.

NOW WE'VE GOT *"WORST CELEBRITY DRIVERS,"* WITH THE FORMAT SOLD TO A HUNDRED TERRITORIES WORLDWIDE.

WE KNOW WHAT WE'RE *DOING*, MR. CONSTANTINE.

I THINK I PREFERRED THE *SNOW*. SO IS THIS SOME NEW FORMAT YOU'RE TRYING OUT: *"NON-CELEBRITY BREAK-IN"*?

YOUR DOOR WASN'T LOCKED. I DIDN'T THINK YOU'D MIND A *CLIENT* MAKING HIMSELF AT HOME.

IS THIS WHERE YOU OFFER ME A GUEST SLOT ON "BRITAIN'S MOST HAUNTED"?

THAT'S NOT SUCH A BAD *GUESS*, MR. CONSTANTINE...

"WE CALL IT 'DARK ENTRIES.' WE'RE CONFIDENT IT'S ANOTHER RATINGS *SMASH*."

"THE CENTRAL CONCEPT IS *FEAR* AND HOW WE COPE WITH IT. THIS, WE FEEL, GIVES THE SHOW AN EDUCATIONAL SLANT. A HOUSE, ITS FRONT DOOR LOCKFAST. ROOMS AND CORRIDORS ALMOST WITHOUT NUMBER."

"RUNNING WATER, A WORKING KITCHEN. HOT FOOD DELIVERED DAILY BY DUMB-WAITER. **NO** CONTACT WITH THE **OUTSIDE WORLD.**

"EVERYTHING MONITORED... **ABSOLUTELY** EVERYTHING."

SO IT'S YOUR BASIC **HAUNTED HOUSE** SCENARIO?

MORE LIKE AGATHA CHRISTIE, "AND THEN THERE WERE NONE." A **GAME** IS BEING PLAYED, MR. CONSTANTINE.

"THERE ARE CONTESTANTS. SIX OF THEM. YOUNG AND IMPRESSIONABLE, EACH ONE A STRANGER TO THE OTHERS. THEY HAVE BEEN CHOSEN WITH A CERTAIN AMOUNT OF CARE: DIFFERENT *PERSONALITIES*, DIFFERENT *STRENGTHS*, DIFFERENT *WEAKNESSES*.

"WE CONTROL THE HOUSE, MR. CONSTANTINE.

"IT HAS BEEN DESIGNED WITH *ONE* THING IN MIND.

"FEAR."

16

"BUT THERE ARE CONSOLATIONS, TOO. AND ONE *BIG* PRIZE..."

"...LOTS OF SECRET TUNNELS AND ROOMS TO BE FOUND, LOTS OF EXPLORING FOR THE *BRAVE* AND THE *AMBITIOUS.*

"AND BEHIND ONE DOOR AND ONE DOOR *ONLY*...

"...AN *EXTRAORDINARY* PRIZE, AWAITING THE WINNER."

THANKS, I'LL BE SURE TO *TUNE OUT.*

FOR THE *FEE* I'M PREPARED TO OFFER, MR. CONSTANTINE, I HOPE YOU'LL MANAGE TO BE MORE *POSITIVE.*

YOUR REPUTATION IS NOT QUITE THE *SECRET* YOU THINK IT.

I'VE HEARD YOU CALLED A *"PARANORMAL INVESTIGATOR."* A NUMBER OF INDEPENDENT PRODUCERS HAVE EVEN PITCHED IDEAS TO ME ABOUT YOU WITHOUT YOU EVER BEING AWARE OF IT, BUT NOTHING FELT QUITE RIGHT...UNTIL *NOW.*

YOU WANT ME TO HELP YOU SCARE A BUNCH OF FAME-HUNGRY *KIDS?*

THAT'LL BE GOOD FOR THE RATINGS.

ABSOLUTELY, BUT ALL THE SAME...

WHAT?

I'D VALUE YOUR ADVICE. ADVERTISERS WOULDN'T LIKE IT IF SOMETHING WENT WRONG.

WHAT COULD POSSIBLY GO WRONG...?

This morning I saw the burning man again.

BUT IS IT REALLY MORNING? NO WAY OF KNOWING. NO WINDOWS TO LOOK OUT OF. NO SUNSHINE, NO SOUNDS OF RAIN. WE SLEEP WHEN WE'RE TIRED, DAY OR NIGHT.

HE NEVER CRIES OUT. ONLY EVER SHOWS HIMSELF TO ME.

I THINK HE'S THE SCARIEST, BUT THEN I'M THE ONLY ONE WHO SEES HIM.

ISHMAEL'S THE OLDEST HERE; THINKS HE HAS TO BE BRAVE ON OUR BEHALF.

BUT THE GHOST CAR SCARES HIM. WHEN HE TALKS ABOUT IT, I SEE THE FEAR IN HIS EYES.

ALICE IS IN A WORLD OF HER OWN. SAYS THERE'S A BIG BIRD, KEEPS SWOOPING DOWN ON HER, BEAK SHARP AS A RAZOR.

THE SCARS ON HER ARMS WEREN'T CARVED BY ANY BEAK...

TOLD HER I'D SWAP FOR MY BURNING MAN ANY DAY.

I LIKE **JUDE**. THERE'S THAT WHIFF OF DANGER ABOUT HIM. HE'S FROM LONDON, SAME AS ALICE.

HE WON'T TELL US WHAT'S HAUNTING HIM, BUT WE KNOW THERE'S SOMETHING. HE SEEMS MORE EMBARRASSED THAN SCARED.

WHEN JUDE HEARD I'M FROM NOTTINGHAM HE KEPT WINDING ME UP, TELLING ME FOREST ARE CRAP. HE'S A CHELSEA FAN. PROBABLY A HOOLIGAN.

HE'S JUST LOOKING FOR A REACTION, STEPH. DON'T GIVE HIM THE SATISFACTION.

THEY ALL CALL ME STEPH RATHER THAN *STEPHANIE*. ISHMAEL SAYS HE USED TO VISIT NOTTINGHAM ON BUSINESS. HE LOOKS AT ME FUNNY SOMETIMES.

HE THINKS MAYBE WE'VE MET BEFORE.

I KNOW WHAT HE MEANS.

SAME WITH JUDE AND ALICE. STRANGERS, BUT NOT QUITE.

AKIKO CAME OVER HERE FROM TOKYO. SHE DOESN'T SAY MUCH. STILL SPEAKS BETTER ENGLISH THAN JUDE.

WHEN SHE TOLD US ABOUT THE NEEDLES, JUDE JOKED THAT SHE WAS A JUNKIE.

WAY SHE JUST SITS THERE FOR HOURS, MAYBE SHE IS.

DOESN'T SEEM TO BOTHER TOM. HE TALKS TO HER CONSTANTLY, WHETHER SHE'S LISTENING OR NOT.

TOM'S A YANK, ALL THE WAY FROM SEATTLE. PACIFIC NORTHWEST, HE SAYS. MISSES HIS COMPUTER MORE THAN HIS LOVED ONES.

THE OLD WOMAN ISN'T ANYONE HE KNOWS.

SHE'S JUST THERE TO SCARE THE SHIT OUT OF HIM.

THEY WANT TO SCARE US OFF, THEY'VE GOT TO TRY HARDER.

TOO RIGHT.

HEAR THAT, VIEWERS?

WANT TO SEE US *SHITTING* OURSELVES, YOU'RE GOING TO HAVE TO RATCHET IT UP!

BUT THE BIRD, IT SEEMS SO REAL...COULD THEY BE MESSING WITH OUR HEADS?

YOU MEAN DRUGS?

WE EAT AND DRINK, DON'T WE?

WE CERTAINLY DO.

BE EASY FOR THEM TO TAMPER WITH IT.

NOT ENOUGH FOR MY LIKING. THIS STUFF'S WEAK AS PISS.

NOW HEAR THIS, ENGLAND! WE. ARE. NOT. FUCKING. SCARED!!

BUT WE ARE. SOME OF US ARE PETRIFIED. WE WANT OUT, AND THAT MEANS FINDING THE SECRET ROOM.

IT MEANS
FINDING
A WAY IN.

CLUES
LEADING
US THERE.

PAST ANY
TRAPS,
DODGING
PITFALLS.

KNOWING
WHO WE
CAN TRUST.

IT'S QUITE A SETUP, MATTY.

I LIKE TO THINK SO.

AND PUNTERS ACTUALLY *WANT* TO BE STUCK IN THERE?

BECOMING CELEBRITIES IN THE PROCESS. WATCHED BY MILLIONS.

AND THE HANGAR HERE, IT'S NOT BUILT ON THE SITE OF A CEMETERY OR SOMETHING?

AUTHOR... PERSON... ONLY

YOU'RE THINKING OF THE FILM "POLTERGEIST"?

IF YOU'D SAID "YES," I COULD'VE COLLECTED MY CASH AND HOOFED IT.

I FEAR IT MAY NOT BE QUITE THAT SIMPLE. HOW ARE THE DARLINGS, BIANCA?

BEHAVING THEMSELVES. YOU MUST BE THE EXORCIST.

MAX VON SYDOW, AT YOUR SERVICE.

MAYBE IF WE SHOW MR. CONSTANTINE SOME OF THE FOOTAGE...?

ALL SET.

ISHMAEL THINKS THERE'S A CAR, RACING TOWARDS HIM.

AKIKO'S SEEING NEEDLES, STICKING UP FROM THE FLOOR.

AND HER?

STEPHANIE. IF SHE CLOSES HER EYES, THE BURNING MAN CAN'T GET HER.

AND *NONE* OF THIS IS YOUR DOING?

WE WEREN'T DUE TO START SCARING THEM UNTIL TONIGHT. FIRST WEEK IN THE HOUSE IS FOR ACCLIMATIZATION. THEN THEY STARTED SEEING THINGS, TALKING ABOUT IT.

SO BRING THEM OUT.

BUT THE RATINGS ARE DYNAMITE! AND NOW YOU'RE HERE...

MASS PSYCHOSIS...TEEN HYSTERIA...THEY'RE GIVING YOU JUST WHAT YOU ASKED OF THEM.

YOU'RE SAYING WE DO NOTHING? JUST LEAVE THEM TO FESTER?

NO NEED TO SOUND SO ENTHUSIASTIC.

THERE'S STUFF I COULD DO: SOME RITES, A FEW SPELLS AND INCANTATIONS. MIGHT CLEAR THE AIR A BIT. AND IF NOT, WE'LL TRY FENG SHUI.

I TOLD YOU THIS WAS A MISTAKE! THE MAN'S A COMPLETE FRAUD!

YOU SCARE KIDS FOR A LIVING... ANY CHANCE SOMEONE ON THE SHOW HAS THEIR OWN AGENDA?

OUR STAFF HAVE BEEN VETTED AND THE MANSION'S SECURE.

SHE REMINDS ME OF SOMEONE...

I THOUGHT SHE WAS YOUR TYPE; SAW IT STRAIGHT AWAY.

AND WHAT TYPE'S THAT THEN, LOVE?

THE DAMSEL IN DISTRESS.

SHOW ME THE TAPES AGAIN, AND ANY MORE YOU'VE GOT LIKE THEM. I'M ASSUMING YOU PSYCH-TESTED THE POOR SODS BEFORE LOCKING THEM UP: I WOULDN'T MIND SEEING THAT STUFF, TOO.

THEY WEREN'T CRAZY WHEN WE PUT THEM INSIDE, MR. CONSTANTINE.

DOESN'T MEAN THEY'RE NOT CRAZY NOW, MATTY. AND I'LL NEED BIANCA TO DO SOMETHING FOR ME.

WHAT?

MUG OF YOUR STRONGEST ROSIE-LEA, MILK AND TWO SUGARS.

AND IT'S NO GOOD SAYING I'M *SWEET* ENOUGH ALREADY...

WHY WOULD ANYONE WATCH THIS?

3:00

MAKING VOYEURS OF US ALL.

3:45

4:25

REMINDS ME OF BEDLAM. NINETEENTH CENTURY, THE GENTRY WOULD TAKE A SUNDAY PROMENADE AROUND THE INSANE ASYLUM.

IT GAVE THEM A BUZZ.

4:50

THIS LOT VOLUNTEERED, OF COURSE. DOESN'T MAKE IT ANY BETTER.

5:25

DOESN'T MEAN THEY'RE NOT BEING GOT AT.

5:50

DOESN'T MEAN THERE ISN'T SOMEONE PULLING THE STRINGS.

YOU CAN DO AMAZING THINGS WITH CGI THESE DAYS.

IF IT WERE *CGI*, WE'D BE ABLE TO SEE WHAT THE CONTESTANTS SEE.

UNLESS SOMEONE'S TAMPERED WITH THE CAMERAS. CHEERS, LOVE.

ANY *PROGRESS*, MR. CONSTANTINE?

SHE'S AN ICE MAIDEN, THAWING MAY TAKE A WHILE.

I MEANT WITH THE--

ONLY THING YOU CAN DO IS SHUT THE GAME DOWN, GO IN THERE YOURSELF AND CHECK THE PLACE OUT. DRINK WHAT THEY DRINK, EAT WHAT THEY EAT. WAIT TO SEE IF *YOU* GET THE WILLIES.

BUT IF WE *CAN'T* SHUT THE GAME DOWN...?

TELL ME YOU'RE NOT THINKING WHAT I *KNOW* YOU'RE THINKING.

AND AFTER YOU'VE DONE THAT, MAYBE YOU CAN LET *ME* IN ON THE SECRET, TOO.

IT'LL MEAN A BIGGER *FEE*, OF COURSE. YOU MAY EVEN BE THE ONE TO FIND THE *TREASURE*...

THE VIEWERS WILL LOVE IT: A SURPRISE *NEW CONTESTANT* ENTERS THE HAUNTED MANSION.

"LADIES AND GENTLEMEN: *JOHN* FROM *LIVERPOOL!*"

41

TEN...NINE... EIGHT...

JOHN FROM LIVERPOOL, THAT'S ME. STILL TIME TO BACK *OUT*, THOUGH...

SEVEN... SIX...FIVE...

CAN'T EVEN TAKE MY BLOODY *CIGGIES* WITH ME: BLOODY GOVERNMENT BLOODY RULES. THINGS COULD GET MESSY, EVEN WITH AN ADDICT'S SUPPLY OF NICOTINE PATCHES.

FOUR... THREE... TWO...

MY SUITCASE HAS ALREADY GONE IN: ENOUGH FOR A COUPLE OF DAYS. DOESN'T MEAN I CAN'T BACK OUT. HAND KEENE BACK HIS CASH AND THE EXTRA CHEQUE...THE CHEQUE WITH ALL THOSE LOVELY *ZEROES*...

TOP OF THE WORLD, MA.

ACTION!

HE'S GOING IN NOW! BOY, ARE THE HOUSEMATES IN FOR A TREAT! JOHN, A FUN-LOVING SCOUSER WHO WORKS AS A MUSIC PROMOTER...

MUSIC PROMOTER WAS MY IDEA...NOT SO SURE NOW.

NOT SURE ABOUT *ANY* OF THIS, EXCEPT ONE THING.

THE GIRL CALLED STEPHANIE... SPITTING IMAGE OF *HELEN CAWDOR.*

NOT HER, OF COURSE, JUST LOOKS LIKE HER...

THING IS, I WAS TOO LATE TO SAVE HELEN. MAYBE THE BIG GUY'S GIVING ME ANOTHER CHANCE...

GOOD TO SEE A NEW FACE, MATE.

JUST THAT I WAS HOPING FOR A BIRD, NO OFFENSE.

GOOD NEWS IS, STEPHANIE'S HEAD'S STILL ATTACHED TO HER NECK...

TOLD YOU I COULD DO IT. HE WENT IN OF HIS OWN FREE WILL. AND SIGNED THE WAIVER.

SO NOW THE FUN REALLY BEGINS...

JUBBLY BUBBLY! SOMEONE UP THERE *LIKES* US!

DON'T SUPPOSE YOU BROUGHT ANY *SMOKES*?

GOT PLENTY OF *THESE*, THOUGH.

SO WHAT'S HAPPENING ON THE *OUTSIDE*?

YOU KNOW THE RULES, STEPH: WE'RE NOT ALLOWED TO KNOW.

BUT NOW THAT JOHN'S BEEN PARACHUTED IN...

YEAH, FUNNY *THAT*. YOU'RE NOT A PLANT OR SOMETHING?

WHAT YOU SEE IS WHAT YOU GET. *CHEERS*, FOLKS.

WELCOME TO THE NUT-HOUSE.

GEEK HOUSE, MORE LIKE, WITH *YOU* IN IT, TOMMY BOY.

WHAT IS YOUR OCCUPATION, MR. CONSTANTINE?

IT'S *JOHN*. AND I'M IN THE MUSIC BIZ.

INTERESTING.

SHE COULD ALMOST BE RELATED... HELEN'S *COUSIN* MAYBE...

NOT REALLY. I PUT ON GIGS AND CLUB NIGHTS. NORTHEAST MOSTLY; NOWHERE YOU'D KNOW. SEEM TO *KNOW* YOU FROM SOMEWHERE THOUGH.

THAT TENDS TO HAPPEN IN HERE. SAME WITH ME AND ISHMAEL, JUDE AND ALICE...

IT'S LIKE WE'RE *CONNECTED* IN SOME WAY.

WE'RE THE *CHOSEN*, STEPH. AND WHEN WE GET OUT OF HERE, WIN OR LOSE, WE'LL BE THE BIGGEST BLOODY CELEBS IN *BRITAIN!*

IF NO ONE DIES OF *FRIGHT* FIRST.

YEAH, THERE MIGHT BE A SCARE OR TWO, BUT THE SHOW'S NOT GOING TO LET ANYTHING HAPPEN TO US. WE'D SUE THEIR *ARSES* OFF.

DO YOU EVER GET USED TO BEING WATCHED ALL THE TIME?

WE LIVE IN *BRITAIN,* JOHN. MORE *C.C.T.V.* ON THE STREETS THAN ANY OTHER COUNTRY IN THE WORLD.

AKIKO DOESN'T SOUND BRITISH.

MY HOME IS TOKYO.

SO HOW DID YOU FIND OUT ABOUT THE SHOW? READ ABOUT IT ON THE WEB?

YES... IT MUST BE SO.

AND THE REST OF YOU?

WHAT'S WITH THE QUESTIONS, NOSY BOY? YOU TRYING TO PSYCH US OUT? MAYBE YOU *ARE* A FUCKING MOLE!

JUST CURIOUS.

HELL HAPPENED?

FUSE, MAYBE.

THERE'S A TORCH IN ONE OF THE DRAWERS.

THIS ONE, YOU MEAN?

IS EVERYONE ALL RIGHT? NOTHING TO WORRY ABOUT, AKIKO?

FUSEBOX IS ON THE WALL ABOVE THE WASHING MACHINE.

LOOKS OKAY TO ME.

AKIKO? JOHN, FLASH THAT THING THIS WAY, WILL YOU?

CRAP, WHERE IS SHE?

MAYBE SHE WAS SCARED YOU'D COP A FEEL.

YOUR FIRST SHOT BETTER *KILL* ME, GEEK BOY.

ENOUGH, TOM. GO FIND AKIKO.

IN THE DARK?

SO MUCH FOR MACHO MAN. SCARED OF HIS OWN *SHADOW*.

LOOK WHAT I'VE FOUND...

ANYONE GOT A LIGHT?

USE ONE OF THE COOKER'S RINGS.

WE'LL GO IN GROUPS OF TWO, BE QUICKER FINDING HER.

LONG AS I'M NOT WITH *FRANK BRUNO* HERE.

YOU CAN GO WITH ALICE. TOM, YOU'RE WITH ME.

THOUGHT YOU AND ISHMAEL WERE SUPPOSED TO HAVE THIS "CONNECTION."

DOESN'T MEAN HE *LIKES* ME.

MIGHT AS WELL MAKE OURSELVES COMFORTABLE.

WHAT ABOUT AKIKO?

YOU GO IF YOU WANT. ME, I'M HAPPY WHERE I AM. THOSE LIGHTS WENT OUT FOR A *REASON.*

WHAT REASON?

THE FUSEBOX IS *FAKE,* NO WIRES GOING IN OR OUT. POWER IN THIS PLACE IS CONTROLLED FROM OUTSIDE. DON'T TELL ME YOU'VE FORGOTTEN THE *GAME* WE'RE PLAYING HERE?

STILL, GIVES US THE CHANCE TO GET *ACQUAINTED.* YOUR HEALTH.

TINK

I HATE
NEEDLES.

EVER SINCE MY FIRST
INOCULATION. THE PUNCTURE
WOUND WAS SLOW TO HEAL.
INFECTION SET IN.

THERE WAS A SMELL
OF DEATH IN MY
BEDROOM AS THE
FEVER TOOK HOLD.

WHENEVER I CLOSED
MY EYES, I SAW COLORS.
PURPLES AND REDS AND
GREENS. GREEN LIKE THE SEA,
RED LIKE A GEISHA'S LIPSTICK.
ALL OF THIS I REMEMBER.

BUT NOT LAST
WEEK, AND NOT
THE WEEK BEFORE
THAT. MAYBE ALICE
IS RIGHT: WE'VE
BEEN DRUGGED.

MR. CONSTANTINE ASKED EXACTLY THE RIGHT QUESTION: WHAT AM I *DOING* HERE?

'BOUT BLEEDIN' TIME.

I DON'T KNOW ENGLAND. DID I TELL MY PARENTS I WAS COMING?

I'M IN THE DARK ABOUT SO MANY THINGS...

OPEN SESAME!

YOU TRYING TO GET ME SOZZLED?

DUNNO... WOULD IT HELP MY CHANCES?

IN FRONT OF AN AUDIENCE OF *EIGHT MILLION?* GET REAL.

BUT WITH ME UNCONSCIOUS, YOU CAN GO EXPLORING, MAYBE FIND THE SECRET ROOM.

GOOD POINT. SOUNDS SOLID ENOUGH.

SO WHAT BRINGS *YOU* HERE, JOHN? THE FAME? THE TREASURE?

MAYBE THE *COMPANY.* HOW ABOUT YOU?

SOUNDS STUPID, BUT I'M NOT REALLY *SURE* NOW.

MUST'VE KNOWN AT THE AUDITION, THOUGH.

I...DON'T REALLY REMEMBER ANY OF IT. WHOLE THING'S BEEN A BIT OF A BLUR.

MUST'VE MET THE CREW, THOUGH. THE PRODUCER-- MATTHEW KEENE? AND HIS BALL-BUSTING ASSISTANT BIANCA?

WE TALK TO MR. KEENE.

YOU TALK TO HIM?

IN THE THRONE ROOM.

AND WHAT'S THAT WHEN IT'S AT HOME?

IT'S HOW WE COMMUNICATE. HAVEN'T YOU BEEN WATCHING THE SHOW?

NO SIGN OF HER.

HELL ARE YOU UP TO?

JOHN'S PLAYING THE GAME, THAT'S ALL.

COULD BE WHAT AKIKO'S DOING, TOO. OFF ON THE HUNT WHILE WE WASTE TIME TRYING TO TRACK HER DOWN.

MAYBE WE SHOULD ASK OUR MASTERS WHAT'S GOING ON. THIS *THRONE ROOM,* ANYONE GOING TO SHOW ME WHERE IT IS?

DO WE TELL HIM NOW?

PUBLIC SAYS HE SHOULD FIND OUT THE HARD WAY...MEANING MORE FUN FOR *US.*

SO KEENE SUMMONS YOU, AND YOU TROOP ALONG HERE? AND NONE OF YOU MET HIM BEFORE YOU CAME IN, OR AT LEAST YOU DON'T REMEMBER MEETING HIM...

BECAUSE NONE OF YOU REMEMBERS THE AUDITION, OR APPLYING TO BE ON THE SHOW. INTERESTING...

AKIKO CAN'T EVEN REMEMBER COMING TO ENGLAND. TO BE HONEST, SHE'S NOT THE ONLY ONE...

I CAN'T HELP THINKING THAT SOMEBODY SOMEWHERE IS HAVING A LAUGH. ONE WAY TO FIND OUT...

LET US IN, YOU CONNIVING BASTARDS!

ONE CONTESTANT *ONLY* AT A TIME IN THE THRONE-ROOM.

GOT TO BE *ME* THEN, EH?

PROMISE YOU'LL ASK ABOUT *AKIKO.*

TOP OF MY LIST, MATE.

WELL, *SECOND* TOP MAYBE...

ANY CHANCE THE CONDEMNED MAN CAN HAVE A *CIGGIE*?

WHAT MAKES YOU THINK YOU'RE CONDEMNED?

FIGURE OF SPEECH, THAT'S ALL. WHAT MAKES YOU ASK?

YOUR *FANS* ARE INTERESTED. THEY WANT TO KNOW WHAT MAKES YOU TICK.

I'VE HARDLY BEEN HERE FIVE MINUTES.

OUR VIEWERS HAVE *TAKEN* TO YOU, MR. CONSTANTINE.

THAT RIGHT? WELL, THEY CAN SHOVE IT UP THEIR JACKSIES. I'M *OUT*, KEENE.

OUT, MR. CONSTANTINE? THERE *IS* NO OUT, EXCEPT FOR THE SECRET ROOM.

THAT WHERE AKIKO IS?

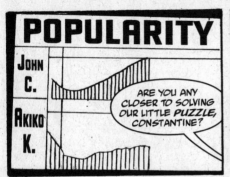

POPULARITY

John C.

Akiko K.

ARE YOU ANY CLOSER TO SOLVING OUR LITTLE *PUZZLE,* CONSTANTINE?

THESE KIDS AREN'T HERE OF THEIR OWN FREE WILL--THAT MUCH I *DO* KNOW. THEY'VE NO IDEA HOW THEY GOT HERE OR WHAT THE HELL'S HAPPENING TO THEM. NOW TELL ME WHERE I CAN FIND AKIKO!

YOU SEEM TO BE GROWING CLOSER TO STEPHANIE. COULD SHE BE YOUR *SOUL-MATE?* TELL US HOW YOU'RE FEELING RIGHT NOW.

KNOW WHAT, KEENE? I CAN'T REALLY PUT IT INTO *WORDS.*

SO *THIS'LL* HAVE TO DO.

HE'S OFF THE SCALE.

POPULARITY

JOHN C.

HE CERTAINLY IS.

WE COULD BRING HIM BACK DOWN TO EARTH WITH A BUMP.

INTERESTING *PHRASE*, UNDER THE CIRCUMSTANCES...

HOUSE CONT

POINT MADE, I RECKON.

I'M SUPPOSED TO BE THE SHOW'S BAD BOY, JOHN. YOU KEEP *THAT* UP AND I'LL BE AFTER A NEW IDENTITY.

FUNNY YOU SHOULD SAY THAT, JUDE-- *IDENTITY'S* THE VERY THING WE NEED TO TALK ABOUT.

POWWOW IN THE REC ROOM?

AND SOME BEER TO WASH DOWN THE BUBBLY.

THEY DIDN'T SAY ANYTHING ABOUT AKIKO?

SORRY, TOM, NOTHING USEFUL. LISTEN, KEENE HAD ME SIGN LOTS OF FORMS BEFORE I CAME IN--ANY OF YOU REMEMBER THE SAME?

MY MIND'S A BLANK.

THAT'S WHAT WORRIES ME, STEPH. TIME TO GET IT OFF YOUR *CHESTS*.

WHAT?

THE VISIONS... THE *THINGS* IN HERE THAT ARE FREAKING YOU *OUT*.

I THOUGHT YOU HAVEN'T BEEN WATCHING THE SHOW.

I NEED YOU LOT TO *TRUST* ME.

SORRY?

A BIT LIKE THE CONFESSIONAL. I NEED TO HEAR EACH STORY IN TURN.

I STILL DON'T GET IT.

ME NEITHER, BUT I'M GOING TO TAKE JOHN AT HIS WORD. WHAT HAVE WE GOT TO LOSE?

MAYBE NOTHING. IT'S WHAT *HE* COULD GAIN THAT WORRIES ME.

FUCK IT. I'M OUTTA HERE!

HE'LL COME ROUND, DON'T WORRY.

MAYBE ONE OF US SHOULD GO AFTER HIM...

SCARED HE'S GOING TO BEAT YOU TO THE LOCKED ROOM, TOM?

66

HOW CAN I TELL THEM?

TELL THEM I'M SCARED OF AN OLD WOMAN'S *HANDBAG?*

SUCH A STUPID THING TO BE SCARED OF. MY GRAN WAS DEAD BEFORE I WAS BORN. NEVER KNEW MY DAD, SO IT WAS JUST THE ONE DEAD GRAN--MUM'S MUM. THEN MUM DID A RUNNER WHEN I WAS SIX.

I KNOW IT'S AN OLD WOMAN'S BECAUSE OF THE SMELLS--TALCUM POWDER AND VIOLETS. THOSE HEAVY SCENTS THEY USE TO DISGUISE THE SMELL OF *WEE.*

CHILDREN'S HOME WASN'T TOO BAD. I'D DO A RUNNER EVERY FEW WEEKS, LIVE ON THE STREETS. STAFF DIDN'T SEEM TO MIND, AND THE KIDS LOVED THAT I BROUGHT BACK CIGS AND HOOCH AND SOMETIMES EVEN A BIT OF BLOW.

68

KNEW WHERE I *WAS* BACK THEN. NOT SO SURE NOW.

STEPH TOLD ME ABOUT THE BURNING MAN. TOLD ME OTHER STUFF, TOO. ALICE'S DREAMS ABOUT THE SWOOPING BIRD; AKIKO AND HER *NEEDLES*.

ISHMAEL KEEPS THINKING A CAR IS COMING FOR HIM. FOR TOM, IT'S SOME OLD DEAR WITH HOLLOWED-OUT EYES. NONE OF IT ENGINEERED BY KEENE, UNLESS THERE'S SOMETHING IN THE WATER.

THERE'S SOMETHING ABOUT STEPH, THOUGH. IT'S NOT JUST THAT SHE REMINDS ME OF HELEN CAWDOR. SHE'S GOT AN *AURA*. MAYBE THAT'S WHAT DREW ME IN HERE--HER SENSE OF *OTHERNESS*...

I *LIKE* HER.

DON'T GET OUT.

DON'T GO THERE.

DON'T LOOK DOWN.

STOP WALKING.

DON'T LOOK.

GORE ROAD FLATS TO BE DEMOLISHED

NO SIGN OF MISSING HELEN

DON'T GO IN THERE.

DON'T
LISTEN.

DON'T DO IT.
DON'T DO IT.
DON'T DO IT.

NOW
YOU'VE GONE
AND DONE IT,
BRIAN...

NOTHING TO DO WITH *ME*, LOVE. TELL YOU WHAT, THOUGH. STEPH'S EXPLAINED ABOUT THE HAUNTINGS--ALL YOUR PERSONAL LITTLE DEMONS.

AND?

AND NOTHING... EXCEPT THAT NOW I'M SEEING THEM, TOO. A CANNIBAL IN MY CASE, GUY I NEVER WANT TO SEE *AGAIN*.

CHRIST, I NEED A DRINK... ANYONE CARE TO *JOIN* ME?

SO TELL US THE STORY, JOHN.

NOT MUCH TO TELL. IT WAS SIX YEARS BACK, GUY I KNEW CALLED *BRIAN McARTHUR.*

ACTUALLY, IT WASN'T BRIAN I KNEW AS MUCH AS HIS *GIRLFRIEND...*

...HELEN CAWDOR. KNEW HER FROM WAY BACK. BUT THEN SHE MET BRIAN. HE WAS A HISTORIAN, DABBLED IN ARCHAEOLOGY-- MYTHS AND LEGENDS.

STARTED RESEARCHING SAWNEY BEAN.

WHO?

"HE LIVED IN THE SCOTTISH COUNTRYSIDE. COULDN'T MAKE MUCH OF A GO OF IT, WHICH MIGHT EXPLAIN WHY HE DID WHAT HE DID."

CANNIBALISM?

SO THE STORY GOES. FAR AS BRIAN WAS CONCERNED, THAT'S ALL IT *WAS,* THOUGH--A STORY.

"BRIAN RECKONED SAWNEY BEAN WAS A *LEGEND*, CONJURED UP AS A COMMENTARY ON THE HIGHLAND CLEARANCES.

"IT'S A HARSH LANDSCAPE. OWNERS RECKONED THEY'D MAKE MORE MONEY FROM SHEEP THAN FROM TENANTS. PEOPLE WERE TURFED OUT OF THEIR HOMES, LIVELIHOODS STRIPPED FROM THEM...

"A LOT OF THEM *STARVED*..."

HUNGER DOES STRANGE THINGS TO A MAN.

I'M STILL NOT SURE I UNDERSTAND...

79

BRIAN GREW OBSESSED. HELEN CALLED ME, SAID SHE WAS WORRIED ABOUT HIM. TOLD ME HE WAS *CHANGING.*

"STARTED EATING HIS STEAKS RARER AND RARER, AND THEN *RAW.* RAW BACON, SAUSAGE, LAMB, LIVER. A NEIGHBOR'S CAT WENT MISSING. SQUIRRELS IN THE GARDEN WITH BITS TORN FROM THEM..."

"PSYCHIATRIST COULDN'T FIND ANYTHING WRONG WITH HIM. HELEN RECKONED IT WENT *BEYOND* THAT, ANYWAY. HER THEORY WAS, SAWNEY HIMSELF HAD TAKEN POSSESSION. BRIAN WASN'T *BRIAN* ANY MORE..."

THE PAIR OF THEM WENT *AWOL.* I TRACKED BRIAN DOWN. HE'D *KILLED* HELEN...

"END OF STORY."

EXCEPT IT *ISN'T*, IS IT?

NOT QUITE, NO.

"HE FELL NINE STORIES. BLOCK WAS DUE FOR DEMOLITION, SO I DRAGGED HIM BACK *INSIDE*."

AND NOW YOU'VE DREAMED ABOUT HIM.

BUT WHEN I OPENED MY EYES, HE WAS STILL *THERE*. SAME AS YOUR BURNING MAN...

YOUR ONCOMING CAR...

YOUR BIG SWOOPING BIRD...

YOUR SPOOKY OLD WOMAN.

SO WHAT DOES IT ALL MEAN?

BRIAN McARTHUR IS **DEAD**. I WATCHED IT HAPPEN. WHATEVER'S GOING ON HERE, DEATH IS **PART** OF IT.

I NEED YOU THINKING ABOUT THAT. ALL THESE PHENOMENA, THEY **MEAN** SOMETHING TO YOU. THEY'RE **NOT** RANDOM.

SO TRY TO REMEMBER. TRY **HARD**.

WHILE **YOU** GO LOOK FOR THE **TREASURE?**

I JUST WANT **OUT** OF HERE, ALICE. I WANT **ALL** OF US OUT OF HERE BEFORE ANYTHING **ELSE** HAPPENS.

HE'S **BETTER** THAN I **EXPECTED**.

KEEP OUT WHEN THE RED LIGHT

I'M GLAD YOU'RE WARMING TO HIM. AFTER ALL...HE'S GOING TO BE **WITH** US FOR A CONSIDERABLE TIME.

THE CANDLES ARE REAL. CANDLES BURN DOWN.

AND THEN THEY NEED TO BE REPLACED. MEANING PEOPLE *COME* HERE.

THEY *RE-LIGHT* THE CANDLES WHEN THEY BLOW OUT.

ALL I HAVE TO DO IS WAIT, AND THEN *FOLLOW*.

FOLLOW THEM OUT OF THE *RABBIT HOLE*...

HAH! THEY LEFT A TORCH HERE.

MEANS THEY'RE ON *MY* SIDE. MEANS I'M *GETTING* SOMEWHERE.

TUNNEL SEEMS TWICE THE LENGTH OF THE HOUSE. MUST BE MY IMAGINATION.

NEVER BEEN SCARED OF TIGHT SPOTS. STAFF AT THE CHILDREN'S HOME USED TO LOCK ME IN THE CUPBOARD.

KKRTCHCK-
KKSSTCHKK KRRCHCH

NEVER GOT THE SATISFACTION OF HEARING *ME* BEG...HELL'S THAT *NOISE?*

KRRCHCH

SOUNDS LIKE THERE'S A GLITCH IN THE *MACHINERY*...OR...

KKRTCH

WHAT THE HELL IS *THAT?*

KSSTCH

KKRCH

SKKRCH

EEYYAAH!!

RESULT.

KEEP OUT WITH THE RED LIGHT

AND ONE OF OUR *OWN* EFFECTS, FOR A CHANGE...

ANY SIGN OF LITTLE AKIKO?

SHE'S SITTING IN THE DARK.

WELL, WE CAN'T HAVE *THAT*, CAN WE?

I REMEMBER THE TRAIN HOME FROM SCHOOL. THE *UNDERGROUND* TRAIN. SOMETIMES THE CARRIAGES WOULD BE PLUNGED INTO DARKNESS. AND THEN...

THE MEN IN THEIR BUSINESS SUITS, THE SALARY-MEN. GOOD AT THEIR BUSINESS, LITTLE WIVES WAITING FOR THEM AT HOME.

I PRAY THE
DARKNESS
DOESN'T
COME.

88

I LET THEM KNOW: KEEP YOUR FILTHY HANDS TO YOURSELVES!

BUT THEN THE LIGHTS GO OUT, AND THE TOUCHING BEGINS...

I KNOW WHAT THEY'RE THINKING...

I KNOW WHY THEY DO IT...

I KNOW WHAT TO DO...

I KNOW WHAT TO DO.

I *EMBRACE* THE DARKNESS.

I EMBRACE THE LIGHT...

INTERESTING...

AND NOT *OUR* DOING.

THE LIGHT IS OURS, BIANCA.

BUT *THAT'S* NOT WHAT SHE'S REACTING TO, IS IT?

I THINK SHE'S STARTING TO REMEMBER.

SHE'S GOOD FOR *WEEKS* YET.

NEVERTHELESS... SAY THERE'S SOMETHING IN THERE WE DON'T KNOW ABOUT, SOMETHING WE DIDN'T *COUNT* ON.

AN EMPATH? WELL, CONSTANTINE'S--

THIS ALL STARTED BEFORE HE CAME IN. MAYBE HE'S NOT THE *ONLY* ONE WITH A TOUCH OF OTHERNESS...

IT COULDN'T HAPPEN.

NOT UNLESS THERE'S A *CONNECTION*... A DEGREE OF SEPARATION. IT WOULD EXPLAIN CONSTANTINE'S FEAR OF SAWNEY BEAN.

JUDE'S ON THE MOVE AGAIN.

I'M DRAWN TO STEPH, BUT I CAN SEE WHY SHE'D PREFER JOHN. ALL MY LIFE, I'VE BEEN LOSING OUT TO GUYS LIKE HIM: SELF-CONFIDENT, CHARISMATIC, PLAIN BLOODY *COCKY*.

THE HOUSE I GREW UP IN HAD AN ATTIC. WE REACHED IT BY A LADDER. YOU TUGGED ON A ROPE AND THE LADDER CAME SLIDING DOWN. I USED TO TELL MILLIE, WATCH IT DOESN'T CHOP YOUR *HEAD* OFF.

MILLIE USED TO LET ME PLAY WITH HER, EVEN THOUGH I WAS FIVE YEARS OLDER THAN HER.

AKIKO, IS THAT *YOU?*

WE'D HAVE TEA PARTIES WITH HER TEDDY BEARS. SHE WAS MUMMY, I WAS DADDY. OR WE'D PLAY GAMES OF TAG AND LEAP-FROG AND HIDE AND SEEK...

JUDE? STOP MUCKING ABOUT.

IT WAS THAT BLOODY *BEAR'S* FAULT.

ISHY, YOU SAID A BAD WORD!

IT FELL OUT OF YOUR BACKPACK ONTO THE SIDEWALK. AND WHEN YOU WENT TO PICK IT UP, YOU KICKED IT INTO THE ROAD. WE WERE ON OUR WAY HOME FROM CAROLYN'S BIRTHDAY PARTY.

I'D PROMISED I'D GO FETCH YOU, WALK YOU HOME. IT WASN'T EVEN A MILE. BUT I WASN'T WATCHING.

"YOU WERE WATCHING THE *WRONG GIRL!*"

SKREEEEE

I WAS WATCHING THE WRONG GIRL. I NEVER FORGAVE MYSELF FOR THAT, MILLIE...NEVER. HONEST TO GOD.

I KNOW THAT, ISHY. I'M SORRY IT WAS ALL SO BAD.

DO WE NEED TO HOLD **HANDS** OR ANYTHING?

IT'S NOT A BLOODY **SEANCE.** ALL WE'RE DOING IS **TALKING.** SO WHY DON'T YOU START.

ME?

HOW LONG HAVE YOU BEEN IN ENGLAND, TOM?

NOT LONG. YOU COULD SAY I'M IN TRANSIT.

TRANSIT TO WHERE?

JAPAN. TO **STUDY.**

WHAT'S YOUR FIELD, TOM?

YOU MEAN LIKE *AVATARS?* ONLINE VERSIONS OF OURSELVES?

I DON'T USE COMPUTERS MUCH, PREFER TO GET MY INFORMATION THE *OLD FASHIONED* WAY...

TV?

NEWSPAPERS.

WHAT'S HAPPENING TO US, JOHN?

I THINK YOUR MINDS HAVE BEEN *WIPED.* NOT SURE WHY.

OUR MINDS...BUT NOT *YOURS?*

FAR AS I CAN TELL.

101

YOU'RE A *MOLE*.

GOT IT IN ONE.

NOT A *MUSIC PROMOTER?* CLUB NIGHTS IN THE NORTHEAST...?

BUT I DO A PRETTY MEAN '80s *MIX-TAPE*—CURE, SMITHS, COCTEAUS.

I *KNEW* THERE WAS SOMETHING ABOUT YOU!

JUST TOO POLITE TO *SAY,* EH, TOM? I'D PROBABLY PUT SOME *DIRE STRAITS* ON *YOUR* TAPE...

"TEARS FOR FEARS...

"MADNESS..."

...AND ERASURE. WELCOME *BACK*, ISHMAEL.

WHERE'VE YOU *BEEN?* CONSTANTINE HERE IS A GODDAMNED *MOLE.* SAYS THAT FUCKER KEENE HAS WIPED OUR MEMORIES.

THEN HOW COME I REMEMBER MY *SISTER?*

HE MEANS *RECENT* MEMORIES-- HOW WE GOT HERE, WHY THE HELL WE VOLUNTEERED IN THE FIRST PLACE.

MAYBE WE *DIDN'T* VOLUNTEER. MAYBE WE WERE *DRUGGED*, SNATCHED FROM THE STREET.

NOT SURE *PRESS-GANGING'S* ACCEPTABLE THESE DAYS, EVEN FOR THE SAKE OF GOOD TELEVISION. ON THE *OTHER* HAND...

"I LOOKED IN STEPH'S ROOM. NO *CLOTHES*.

"I'M GUESSING IT'S THE SAME FOR *ALL* OF YOU. DON'T YOU FIND THAT A BIT *ODD?*"

105

MAYBE WE ALL SCREWED UP OUR LIVES SOMEWHERE AND THIS IS THE PUNISHMENT. THE PUNISHMENT...OR THE *CURE*.

THAT WOULD MAKE US *PRISONERS.*

WHAT MAKES YOU THINK WE'RE *NOT?*

CAN *YOU* HELP US, JOHN? IS THERE SOME *EMERGENCY EXIT* WE DON'T KNOW ABOUT?

THAT'S NOT A BAD IDEA! IF WE STARTED A FIRE OR SOMETHING, THEY'D *HAVE* TO SEND HELP.

EXCEPT...

SPRINKLERS.

FIRE EXTINGUISHERS.

NOT FORGETTING THAT THE SHOW'S DRIVEN BY *RATINGS*, AND SOMETHING TELLS ME OUR WONDERFUL VIEWERS WOULD *RELISH* THE CHANCE TO WATCH US DODGING THE FLAMES.

AND HOW CAN WE TRUST ANYTHING *YOU* SAY, YOU GODDAMNED *JUDAS*?

I'D SAY I'M THE *LEAST* OF YOUR BLOODY PROBLEMS RIGHT NOW!

JOHN'S RIGHT. THE WAY OUT OF HERE IS TO FIND WHAT CONNECTS US. FIGHTING AMONG OURSELVES IS JUST WHAT THEY *WANT*. THIS WHOLE GAME'S ABOUT SETTING US IN OPPOSITION TO EACH OTHER.

I WAS UPSTAIRS. THEY SHOWED ME MY *SISTER*. SHE SEEMED SO REAL, BUT I WAS JUST A KID WHEN SHE DIED.

WAS IT A *CAR ACCIDENT*?

HOW DID *YOU* KNOW?

YOU DREAM ABOUT HEADLIGHTS, A CAR COMING TOWARDS YOU. THESE NIGHTMARES, THEY'RE THINGS WE'RE AFRAID OF...THINGS FROM OUR *PAST*.

SO *TELL* ME, ALICE, JUST WHEN DID A HUGE *BIRD* SWOOP DOWN AND CARRY YOU OFF TO ITS *EYRIE*?

IT MIGHT *NOT* BE AN ACTUAL BIRD.

AN AIRPLANE MAYBE...

OR ANYTHING *SHARP*, ANYTHING THAT CAN *CUT*.

YES...MAYBE...

WHAT DO *YOU* THINK, JOHN?

I THINK I'D LIKE IT BETTER IF WE WEREN'T ALWAYS BEING *SPIED ON*.

SPIED ON BY *YOUR EMPLOYERS*, YOU MEAN.

WHY *DID* THEY SEND YOU IN HERE ANYWAY?

THE HOUSE IS SUPPOSED TO SCARE YOU, BUT NOT THE WAY IT'S BEEN *DOING*. KEENE AND HIS CREW WANT TO KNOW WHAT'S GOING ON.

THE DREAMS, THE NIGHTMARES... NOTHING TO DO WITH THE *SHOW*. THEY'D HAVE PULLED THE *PLUG*, BUT THE RATINGS HAVE BEEN *DYNAMITE*.

WELL, THAT'S *SOMETHING,* I SUPPOSE...

ON THE OUTSIDE, I'M A SORT OF *DETECTIVE.*

CRASHH

AND ON THE *INSIDE,* YOU'RE A NINE-STONE *WEAKLING.*

GOOD THAT YOU CAN KEEP A SENSE OF *HUMOR,* SWEETHEART.

WHAT MAKES YOU THINK THE ONLY CAMERAS THEY HAVE ARE THE ONES WE CAN *SEE?*

SOME KIND OF *BUG.* SOMETHING TELLS ME IT WON'T BE THE *ONLY* ONE.

IF YOU WERE REAL, I'D EAT YOU RAW. BETTER BE SOME BLOODY *FOOD* WAITING IN THIS SECRET BLOODY ROOM.

GOOD NEWS IS, THERE'S NOT ROOM IN HERE FOR HANDBAG CRAP TO START RAINING DOWN ON ME...

AW, HELL...

IT IS SIMPLE *COWARDICE,* AKIKO, WHICH DRAGS YOU FROM THE DARKNESS. THE SAME COWARDICE YOU SHOWED ON THE JOURNEY TO AND FROM SCHOOL.

NOT STANDING UP FOR *YOURSELF,* NOT TELLING THOSE MEN TO THEIR FACES THAT YOU THOUGHT THEM THE LOWEST FORM OF LIFE. GOING HOME AND PUTTING ON YOUR *DISGUISE.*

TRYING TO BE SOMEONE ELSE...*ANY-ONE* ELSE.

YOUR GRANDMOTHER DIED A DIABETIC. HER SYRINGE IS STILL IN THE BATHROOM, HEAVY AND METALLIC WITH A CLEAR GLASS BODY.

HEY, AKIKO!

FANCY MEETING YOU HERE...

PHISSH

WHAT CAN I DO FOR YOU, CONSTANTINE?

THOUGHT YOU'D WANT A *PROGRESS REPORT*, KEENE.

..SO YOU *HAVE* MADE SOME *PROGRESS?*

I'VE DONE THE *SHERLOCK HOLMES* THING, COME TO A FEW *DEDUCTIONS.*

AND WHAT MIGHT *THOSE* BE?

I NEED A *CIGARETTE*, KEENE. SEND ONE IN AND I'LL TELL YOU WHAT I KNOW.

BIG OF YOU.

MY SIDE OF THE BARGAIN, CONSTANTINE.

WHEN YOU'VE ELIMINATED THE PROBABLE, WHATEVER'S *LEFT* HAS TO BE *TRUE.* LIKE MY THINKING, KEENE?

GO ON.

THEY'RE *DEAD,* AREN'T THEY? ALL SIX OF THEM--NOT *ONE* OF THEM'S ACTUALLY ALIVE.

TELL ME *WHY* YOU THINK THAT.

DON'T SHIT A SHITTER, KEENE.

HOW ARE YOU GOING TO BREAK THIS NEWS TO THEM? THEY'LL SAY YOU'RE *CRAZY.*

THERE'S A *BIGGER* QUESTION THAN THAT, KEENE. BECAUSE IF THEY'RE *DEAD*, THAT MEANS I'M *NOT* IN ANY REALITY FUCKING *TV SHOW*.

OH, BUT YOU *ARE!* ONE WE'VE BEEN WANTING YOU TO JOIN FOR SOME CONSIDERABLE TIME, ONLY WE COULDN'T THINK OF A WAY YOU'D *ACCEPT*.

BUT YOU *DID* ACCEPT... YOU SIGNED THE CONTRACT, AND THAT MAKES YOU *OURS* FOR THE *DURATION*...

YOU'RE OUR *STAR ATTRACTION*, CONSTANTINE. OUR VIEWERS ARE *BAYING* FOR YOU, *LITERALLY* BAYING.

SO WHAT *ELSE* DO YOUR DEDUCTIONS TELL YOU?

IF THE HOUSEMATES ARE THE *DEAR DEPARTED*, THAT MEANS I'M IN HEAVEN OR HELL. ANY POINT IN ME GUESSING *HEAVEN?*

NONE AT ALL, CONSTANTINE...

SO ALL THAT STUFF YOU TOLD ME...THE TV CHEF... THAT WAS JUST A *STORY?*

A *TRUE* STORY, CONSTANTINE. THE CHEF *BELONGS* TO ME...OR RATHER, TO MY *EMPLOYER.* A *LOT* OF THEM DO-- THE TALENTLESS, THE OPPORTUNISTS, THE BRAZEN--THE *CREAM* OF THE TV SCHEDULES!

ME TELLING THEM THEY'RE IN HELL, REDUCED TO PLAYTHINGS, PIECES IN A DEMON'S GAME. PROBABLY QUALIFIES AS "INTERESTING"...MIGHT EVEN STRETCH TO "MIND-BLOWING."

LAST THING I WANT IS PEOPLE AROUND ME WITH BLOWN MINDS. MAKES *SENSE* NOW, THOUGH...

BRIAN MCARTHUR...*HE* MUST HAVE SEEN THE RESEMBLANCE, KNEW I'D BE *INTRIGUED.* KNEW IT MIGHT BE ENOUGH OF A SNARE.

STEPH, SPITTING IMAGE OF MY FRIEND *HELEN,* THE FRIEND I COULDN'T SAVE.

HOW DO I TELL THEM? *WHAT* DO I TELL THEM? WHEN? "HEY GUYS, ANYONE SMELL *CHARNEL* AROUND HERE?"

NEVER BEEN MY *STRONG SUIT,* DIPLOMACY...

THE GENTLE TOUCH.

BEDSIDE MANNER.

SO...WHY WIPE THEIR MEMORIES? TO MAKE THE GAME ALL THE *CRUELER* WHEN THEY FINALLY REALIZE THE *TRUTH?*

WALKED RIGHT INTO IT THOUGH, DIDN'T YOU? KNEW AT THE BACK OF YOUR MIND THERE WAS MORE TO IT, BUT THAT DIDN'T STOP YOU. COLD HARD CASH AND THE MEMORY OF NEVER QUITE GETTING TO SHAG HELEN CAWDOR, AND YOU'RE SIGNED UP FOR THE DURATION.

WAY *IN* MEANS THERE'S A WAY *OUT*. AND WHAT ABOUT THAT SECRET ROOM? IF IT REALLY EXISTS, WHAT'S *INSIDE*?

CHRIST, *LISTEN* TO YOU. WHAT'S THE POINT OF AN ESCAPE HATCH? ONLY THING WAITING OUT THERE IS HELL. HELL AND *BRIAN McARTHUR.*

HIM AND EVERY *OTHER* FUCKER I'VE SENT DOWN HERE.

135

"I TRACKED HIM DOWN. HADN'T LAID EYES ON HIM IN FIVE OR SIX YEARS, BUT HE HADN'T *CHANGED*. DIDN'T SEEM SURPRISED WHEN I RANG THE BELL. LET ME IN, WHISKEY ON HIS BREATH...*THAT* HADN'T CHANGED, EITHER.

"HE USED TO...USED TO *DO* THINGS, TIL THE NIGHT MY MUM PLUCKED UP THE COURAGE TO GRAB ME AND RUN. I NEVER FORGAVE HIM. AND HERE HE WAS, LIVING THE HIGH LIFE WHILE WE GOT BY ON *HANDOUTS*.

"MUM TRIED GETTING MONEY OUT OF HIM, BUT HE ALWAYS HAD SOME EXCUSE. YET *HIS* PLACE WAS A *PALACE*.

"*BATHROOM* WAS THE SIZE OF THE PLACE ME AND MUM WERE *LIVING*."

"QUITE THE *ROMANTIC,* WITH ALL THOSE CANDLES AND STUFF..."

"SMART KITCHEN, TOO. NOT THAT THE COOKER LOOKED LIKE IT HAD EVER BEEN *USED*..."

SZZSSSSS

YOUR *BURNING MAN?*

MY FATHER.

AND YOU GOT CAUGHT IN THE EXPLOSION?

I RAN OUTSIDE... DIDN'T KNOW WHAT I WAS DOING...RAN STRAIGHT INTO THE ROAD...

IF I'M IN HOSPITAL, HOW COME THIS SEEMS SO *REAL?*

BECAUSE IT *IS* REAL. YOU SAID THE FIRST TIME YOU FELT REALLY ALIVE WAS IN BED WITH ME. PROBLEM IS, STEPH, IT'S ALMOST EXACTLY THE *OPPOSITE.*

I...DON'T FOLLOW.

WHEN TWO PEOPLE CONNECT, THERE'S AN *ENERGY* THAT PASSES BETWEEN THEM, LIKE AN EXCHANGE OF LIFE FORCES. IT DIDN'T HAPPEN, STEPH.

YOU'RE SAYING I'M *DEAD?*

YOU **ALL** ARE. AND SOME- HOW YOU'VE ENDED UP TRAPPED IN THIS DAMNED GAMESHOW--BY WHICH I MEAN A GAMESHOW SET UP TO AMUSE THE **DAMNED.** YOU'RE IN HELL, STEPH, WE ALL ARE. AND I'M THE ONLY ONE STILL **LIVING.**

WE'VE MANAGED TO EXPLAIN THE BURNING MAN, BUT THERE'S GOT TO BE SOME CONNECTION TO THE OTHERS. HANG ON, DIDN'T ISHMAEL SAY HE SOMETIMES WENT TO NOTTINGHAM?

AND HE KEEPS BEING HAUNTED BY AN ONCOMING CAR! STEPH, THAT'S **GOT** TO BE IT.

STEPH?

I'M DEAD?

DID YOU NOTICE HOW QUICK YOU JUMPED INTO **BED** WITH ME? YOUR BODY'D NOTED MY **LIFE FORCE,** AND IT **WANTED** SOME.

BUT RIGHT NOW WE HAVE TO CONCENTRATE ON **WHY** YOU'RE HERE. BECAUSE MY HUNCH IS, IF YOU WERE MEANT TO BE IN HELL IN THE FIRST PLACE, THEN THAT'S WHERE YOU'D BE.

140

OUT THERE WITH THE **SPECTATORS**, NOT IN HERE AS PART OF THE GAME. MEANING THERE HAS TO BE A WAY OUT-- AND I THINK IT BEGINS AND ENDS WITH **YOU**, STEPH.

ME?

"ALIVE OR DEAD, STEPH, THERE'S SOME KIND OF **POWER** IN YOU--I CAN **FEEL** IT."

AND THAT MEANS KEENE AND THE OTHERS PROBABLY **KNOW** ABOUT IT. THEY'LL BE WORRIED, STEPH. WE NEED TO WORK FAST...

THE OTHERS... WE NEED TO **TELL** THEM.

BEST THEY DON'T KNOW, NOT JUST YET.

KNOW **WHAT** EXACTLY?

OKAY THEN, CHANGE OF PLAN.

ISHMAEL, OLD BUDDY, WHAT DO YOU REMEMBER ABOUT YOUR LAST TRIP TO **NOTTINGHAM**...?

143

144

147

AKIKO, YOU AND TOM FELT A CONNECTION, BUT YOU LIVED IN TOKYO AND TOM IN SEATTLE. ARE THERE *ANY* CLUES YOU CAN GIVE US, ANYTHING AT *ALL*?

IT HAS BEEN RETURNING TO ME SLOWLY. I HAD ANOTHER SELF. MY OTHER SELF WROTE THINGS ON THE INTERNET...

A *BLOG*?

"I WROTE ABOUT MY DAYS IN TOKYO, MY FEELINGS, ALL SORTS OF THINGS. THERE WERE SITES I VISITED OFTEN. THEY WERE FOR PEOPLE LIKE ME.

"SOME OF THEM PROPOSED SUICIDE PACTS. WE WOULD SHOW THE WORLD OUR CONTEMPT. BUT I HAD *ANOTHER* PLAN.

"THERE WAS AN OLD SYRINGE IN MY PARENTS' BATHROOM, AND BOTTLES OF INSULIN. I PLANNED MY REVENGE."

OH MY GOD! I REMEMBER!

KEEP IT *DOWN*, TOMMY-BOY.

I USED TO SPEND ALL DAY SURFING THE WEB. LOVED JAPANESE CULTURE... LOVED YOUR *BLOG*, AKIKO. AND THEN YOU STOPPED POSTING. I KNEW I HAD TO *DO* SOMETHING.

THERE WASN'T A TRACE OF YOU...NOBODY ONLINE HAD ANY IDEAS...

"ONLY THING I COULD THINK OF WAS COMING TO TOKYO AND *LOOKING* FOR YOU. BUT THAT NEEDED MONEY, AND I WAS *BROKE*.

"EVERYONE IN THE NEIGHBORHOOD KNEW *MRS. KRANTZ* HAD MONEY. KNEW SHE HADN'T TRUSTED A BANK IN HALF A CENTURY."

WELCOME

"THE GUN WAS PLASTIC, CAME WITH A VIDEO GAME I'D GOTTEN TIRED OF.

"SHE WAS ALREADY DEAD. *HEART ATTACK* MAYBE.

"COPS TURNED UP SAME TIME AS THE PARA-MEDICS.

"I DON'T KNOW HOW MANY TIMES THEY *FIRED...*"

FIRED, DO YOU *HEAR* ME?! THE WHOLE *LOT* OF YOU IF I DON'T GET VISUALS IN THE NEXT *TEN SECONDS.*

WHAT ARE THEY *WHISPERING* ABOUT?! CONSTANTINE, YOU LITTLE SHIT, YOU'RE DIGGING A *HOLE* FOR YOURSELF!

"THOUGHT ABOUT SLASHING MY WRISTS, BUT I'D ALREADY TRIED THAT AND MADE A *MESS* OF IT.

"EASIER BY FAR TO JUST STEP OFF THE EDGE, FALL INTO THE *VOID*...

"SWOOP LIKE AN EAGLE!

PITY *I* HAD TO BE WAITING AT THE END OF IT. OF ALL THE BLOODY TOWER-BLOCKS I COULD'VE CHOSEN...

"LOOKED AROUND ME, NO ONE WATCHING. NEVER THOUGHT TO LOOK **UP**..."

LIKE THE PUNCHLINE TO A BAD JOKE.

SORRY ABOUT THAT, JUDE.

YOU **KILLED** ME, YOU FUCKER.

157

TOM WANTS TO FIND HER, AND ENDS UP FINDING SEATTLE'S FINEST INSTEAD.

SO WE'RE ALL CONNECTED-- WHOOPY-FUCKING- *DOO*.

ON TOP OF WHICH, WE HAVE TO CONTEND WITH KNOWING WE'RE DEAD.

DEAD AND PART OF A GAME SHOW IN *HELL*--YOU EXPECT US TO GO *ALONG* WITH THIS SHIT?

BUT IT ALL STARTED WITH *YOU*, STEPH...AND THAT HAS TO *MEAN* SOMETHING...

169

173

CHRIST, THAT HURTS.

HEY! COME *BACK* HERE! I'VE NOT FINISHED WITH YOU!

BITE ME.

LOOKS LIKE WE'VE GOT A NEW *FAVORITE...*

B.Mc.

J.C.

WHATEVER.

174

179

183

194

196

CRAASHH

DRAWBRIDGE RAISED, PORTCULLIS CLOSED...

I WONDER IF THE OTHERS REACHED LIMBO. AND DO THE DEAD REALLY GIVE A SHIT WHERE THEY END UP?

I SHOULD FEEL BAD ABOUT *STEPH*, THOUGH. I KNOW I SHOULD. BUT SHE KILLED HER OLD MAN, AND THESE THINGS HAVE A WAY OF BALANCING OUT.

PAYBACK, YOU MIGHT CALL IT.

THEN AGAIN, MAYBE *NOT*.

MORE VERTIGO CRIME

THE CHILL
AVAILABLE NOW

Written by **JASON STARR**
(Best-selling author of *Panic Attack* and *The Follower*)

Art by **MICK BERTILORENZI**

A modern thriller steeped in Celtic mythology —
a broken-down cop tracks a seductive killer who
possesses the supernatural power known as "the
chill." Can he stop her before her next victim
dies horribly... but with a smile on his face?

THE BRONX KILL
AVAILABLE NOW

Written by **PETER MILLIGAN**
(GREEK STREET)

Art by **JAMES ROMBERGER**

A struggling writer is investigating his Irish cop
roots for his next novel. When he returns home
from a research trip, his wife is missing and finding
her will lead him to a dark secret buried deep in his
family's past.

THE EXECUTOR
AVAILABLE NOW

Written by **JON EVANS**
(Author of *Dark Places* and *Invisible Armies*)

Art by **ANDREA MUTTI**

When a washed-up ex-hockey player is mysteriously
named executor of an old girlfriend's will, he must
return to the small town he left years earlier. There, he
finds a deadly secret from his past that could hold the
key to his girlfriend's murder... if it doesn't kill him first.